KIDS! PICTURE YOURSELF
Making Jewelry

Denise Etchison

Course Technology PTR

A part of Cengage Learning

COURSE TECHNOLOGY
CENGAGE Learning™

Australia • Brazil • Japan • Korea • Mexico • Singapore • Spain • United Kingdom • United States

COURSE TECHNOLOGY
CENGAGE Learning™

Kids! Picture Yourself Making Jewelry

Denise Etchison

Publisher and General Manager, Course Technology PTR:
Stacy L. Hiquet

Associate Director of Marketing:
Sarah Panella

Manager of Editorial Services:
Heather Talbot

Marketing Manager: Jordan Casey

Acquisitions Editor: Megan Belanger

Project Editor: Sandy Doell

Kid Reviewer: Shelby Hiquet

Interior Photography: Tami Blevins

PTR Editorial Services Coordinator:
Erin Johnson

Interior Layout: Jill Flores

Cover Designer: Mike Tanamachi

Indexer: Katherine Stimson

Proofreader: Heather Urschel

For product information and technology assistance, contact us at
Cengage Learning Customer & Sales Support, 1-800-354-9706

For permission to use material from this text or product, submit all requests online at **cengage.com/permissions**

Further permissions questions can be emailed to
permissionrequest@cengage.com

All trademarks are the property of their respective owners.

Library of Congress Control Number: 2008902391

ISBN-13: 978-1-59863-526-3

ISBN-10: 1-59863-526-3

Course Technology
25 Thomson Place
Boston, MA 02210
USA

Cengage Learning is a leading provider of customized learning solutions with office locations around the globe, including Singapore, the United Kingdom, Australia, Mexico, Brazil, and Japan. Locate your local office at: **international.cengage.com/region**

Cengage Learning products are represented in Canada by Nelson Education, Ltd.

For your lifelong learning solutions, visit **courseptr.com**

Visit our corporate website at **cengage.com**

Printed in the United States of America
1 2 3 4 5 6 7 11 10 09

For my daughter Calee Etchison.

Thank you for being you.

ACKNOWLEDGMENTS

A special thanks to my family and friends for their encouragement, support, and love.

Special thanks to my daughter Calee Etchison for your patience and always being there for me.

Sandy Doell, thanks for all your hard work, patience, sense of humor, and working your magic.

Thank you to the following mentors, friends, and inspirations:

Tami Blevins Photography

Shelby Hiquet

Anna Villanyi

Laura Villanyi

Beth Wentz

Melanie Reckas

Indianapolis Art Center

Michele Etchison

Desi Busby

Dustin Etchison

Lucas Etchison

Rex, Dianna, Dan, and Brandon

Apollo, Aspen, Eller, Big Daddy, Patchy, Scotch, Miss Walter, & Cosmo

In memory of Toby. Good Boy!

Thank you to everyone who contributed to the creation of this book: Stacy Hiquet, publisher; Megan Belanger, acquisitions editor; Heather Talbot, manager of editorial services; Jill Flores, layout and design; Heather Urschel, proofreader; Katherine Stimson, indexer; and everyone at Cengage Learning for their cooperation and encouragement.

ABOUT THE AUTHOR

Denise Etchison grew up on a farm in central Indiana, where she always felt an urge to make art. She spent many hours as a child walking the corn rows searching for what some might call ordinary rocks, but she called her "treasures." With a little care and polish, she knew their beauty could be brought out. Early attempts at artwork were created from old fence wire and barn roofing found on the farm.

Until 1996, Denise spent most of her professional life working in retail and merchandising while raising her daughter Calee. Then, by chance, she drove past the Indianapolis Art Center and saw a sign that said "Register Now for Classes." Over the next few years, she embarked on an artistic exploration that took her from ceramics and steel sculpture and finally to her true passion—jewelry design. She was fortunate enough to find encouraging teachers to mentor her in wire wrapping, glass fusing, metalsmithing, and stone inlay, all of these forming the foundation of her training in jewelry fabrication. Lapidary work (the cutting and shaping of stones) and the creation of silver settings (bezels) to place stones in has become her favorite form of design. It allows her to return to the earlier joy she found in collecting rocks and fossils, letting their naturally occurring patterns and geometry inspire her creations.

In 2000, Denise began to give back to the community that encouraged her skills by becoming a jewelry instructor at the Indianapolis Art Center. She built her own home studio in 2003, where she teaches private lessons and workshops. She began to sell her artwork through retail venues and at art fairs. Denise currently conducts workshops and demonstrations in public schools, tailoring her art instruction for kindergarten through high school classes, and mentoring high school interns who serve apprenticeships in her studio. Through teaching and participation in art fairs, Denise has been able to add the element of human interaction so important to inspiring a creative life. Denise loves seeing her students' eyes light up when they master a new skill or speaking to someone who has found inspiration and joy in wearing her jewelry designs.

Denise is the author of *Picture Yourself Making Jewelry and Beading*, published in 2008. She has also had articles published in magazines, including *Fishers/Geist Magazine.*

TABLE OF CONTENTS

Project 1
Forest Fairy Halo

Project 2
Braided Friendship Bracelet

Project 3
Love and Friendship Beads

Project 4
B.F.F. Tag You're It! Necklace

Project 5
Label Holder Necklace

Project 6
Leather Cord and Donut Bead Necklace

Project 7
Memory Wire Bracelet

Project 8
Ribbon and Silk Flower Bracelet

Project 9
Leather Bracelet with Brads

Project 10
Beaded Inspiration Bracelet

Project 11
Wood Decoupage Necklace

Project 12
Colorful Beads and Hemp Cord Necklace

Project 13
Message in a Bottle Necklace

Project 14
Wire Spiral Ring

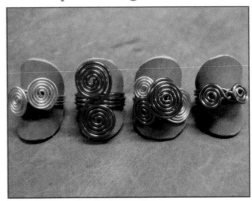

Project 15
Bead Drop Earrings

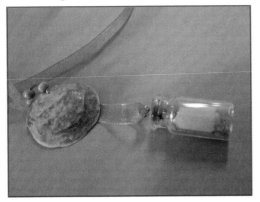

Project 16
Bead Drop Necklace

MESSAGE FROM THE AUTHOR

The jewelry projects in this book are meant to inspire the beginning jewelry artist. Here you will learn the basics of jewelry design and creation; after you work on some of the projects in this book, you'll be able to create your own designs and express your own ideas through art. You will learn to make your own jewelry and wear it as a personal expression of who you are.

Remember these things as you work:

Experimentation is good.

Be happy when you make a mistake! Mistakes are part of the learning process. Many times "mistakes" will become ideas for other designs. You will learn from all of your mistakes.

The techniques described in *Kids! Picture Yourself Making Jewelry* will appeal to both beginning and experienced artists. There's something here for everyone!

My goal is that you will have fun and enjoy making the projects in the book, but I also want to inspire originality in each individual's work. *Art* means the freedom to express yourself in your own way, not just copying what I tell you to do in this book, so use the book as a starting point for your own designs.

Start out with limited tools. Seek inexpensive alternatives, improvise with what you have on hand, or use what is easily obtained. Think "outside the box," which is just another way of saying "be creative," and find new uses for ordinary items.

The projects in this book are arranged, more or less, in order of difficulty. The simple detailed instructions make it easy for you to jump in at any point and complete a project. Or you can start at the beginning and work your way through from simple to more complicated. Project 1, the Forest Fairy Halo, requires only tools you probably already have in your kitchen or workshop. Project 2, Braided Friendship Bracelet, also requires little in the way of tools. Later projects, such as Project 14, the Wire Spiral Ring, require a little more work, more tools, and attention to safety cautions. All the pieces in this book, though, are things you can make today and wear tonight.

All the projects have detailed step by step instructions; you can't go wrong as you work your way through the book. If you are just starting to make jewelry, you will find many useful tips and advice about tools throughout the book.

My hope is to spark your imagination and show you that your creative options are endless.

No matter how long you have been making and designing jewelry, there are always different and new techniques to learn. It is a constant learning process with no end in sight!

It is gratifying to make something yourself and be able to wear it. When you give something you made yourself as a gift, it's personal and special; a part of you went into making it.

There is no wrong. The more you experiment with the projects you'll learn in this book, the more options you will have with your designs.

The projects in this book should be considered as basic instruction, a starting place for your own ideas. Use your imagination and make each design your own by changing the colors or materials.

Denise says:
"Teaching workshops and having a daughter has taught me that kids like to be allowed to be messy, they like things to be easy to understand, and they like to add their own style to the design, I also have learned that kids really like to use a hammer!"

A Word About Tools

You might want to start your own toolbox and put in a few useful items that you will need for other projects in your jewelry making career. Let your friends and family know that you are open to donations of their old tools. Have a birthday coming up? Let everyone know that you are starting a toolbox; they may ask you to provide a wish list. And this is a good one no matter how old you are—let "Santa" know what is on your wish list. Tools do not have to be expensive. Your toolbox can grow over time; you can get more tools as you need them for new projects.

You don't need to buy an actual toolbox. A shoe box works great to hold the tools you'll need for your jewelry projects. Reduce, reuse, recycle!

Make your toolbox a work of art itself. Decorate the shoe box by painting it. Use decoupage glue to add copies of your favorite photos over the painted surface. Keep it simple or go all out by adding stickers, sequins, rhinestones, feathers; or just about anything that makes you happy!

Get your artistic groove on! Paint the handles of your tools bright, funky colors! This will make them easy to keep track of and will make you smile when you use them!

Ask a parent first of course, but following are some places where you can find tools:

Raid the garage workbench. You might offer to help clean and organize the workbench and toolboxes in exchange for a few hand-me-down tools!

Go through old toolboxes and junk drawers.

Visit garage sales and flea markets.

Don't forget craft stores, local hardware stores, and farm supply stores.

The list of tools you'll need for the projects in this book begins on the next page, but here are some additional items you might want to add to your toolbox when you run across them:

Bandages—In case you suffer a little for your art.

Q-Tips—These are good for wiping away excess glue.

Paper towels—You'll need these for clean up.

Tweezers—These come in handy for picking up tiny objects.

Toothpicks—Keep just a couple on hand; they can be used to put glue in the tiniest of places.

Plastic sandwich or snack baggies—These help you keep just about everything, no matter how small, organized.

Old magazines—You need these for decoupage projects.

Tools Used in This Book

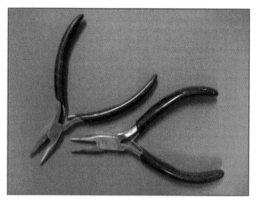

Pliers

Many specialty pliers are available through jewelry supply companies. Before you invest in costly pliers, start with the basics and build from there. Two pair of chain nose pliers, two pair of round nose pliers, and a good pair of cutters. I always keep an old pair of pliers close by to use for certain tasks. I keep a good pair close to use for other tasks.

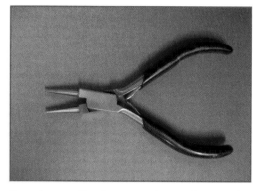

Round nose pliers have round smooth tapered jaws. Use them to make loops and curved bends in wire. Find them at your local arts and craft store or jewelry supply company.

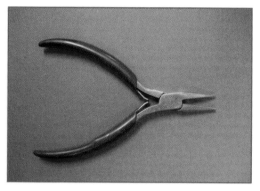

Chain nose pliers have flat smooth tapered jaws. Use these to grip small components. Use them to bend and shape wire and hold small objects. It's good to have at least two pairs on hand. Find these at local arts and craft store or jewelry supply company.

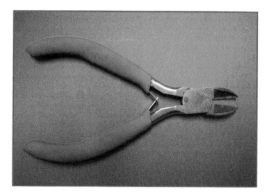

Wire cutters: This is a tool with blades that will cut thick materials. These can easily be found at a hardware store or discount store. You may prefer a pair of smaller wire cutters purchased from an arts and crafts store. They can be found in the jewelry department. These are used to cut the wire for the ring in Project 14.

Markers, pens, and pencils: Keep lots of sizes handy. These are good, not only for marking measurements, but for many other uses. Use them to wrap wire around to make the curls on the Forest Fairy Halo in Project 1. They are also used in Project 14 to make the shank of the ring.

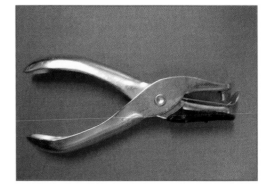

You will find many uses for a 1/16" hole punch! You can purchase this item at many arts and crafts stores. Also check scrapbooking stores.

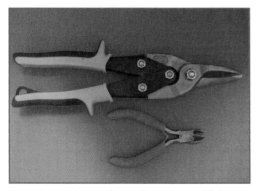

Tin snips are larger than wire cutters with larger cutting blades. You may find wire cutters easier to use because of their smaller size. Check with your parents; they may have an old pair that you can add to your toolbox.

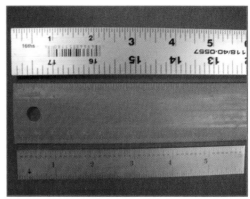

A ruler is a must have! Raid the junk drawer, and go through old school supplies before you resort to buying a new one.

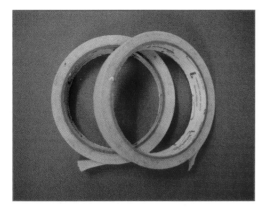

Keep a roll of gift wrapping or masking tape in your toolbox. Use it to hold the ends of the braided friendship bracelet in place, use on the ends of cord to keep beads from sliding off. Be aware of what you are sticking any tape to. You do not want it to take the finish off a piece of furniture. When in doubt, check with an adult.

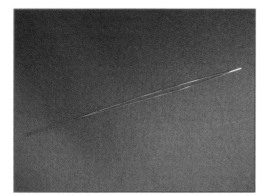

A beading needle is a long flexible needle, usually made from wire. It has a large hole (eye) to place thread or cord through. The beading needle is used in Project 10. It is not sharp like a sewing needle but you do need to be careful with it because it is pointed.

Craft glue is used in many ways; several varieties and brands are available. Check the label to make sure the glue is recommended for the type of project that you are using it for. You can use glue to keep items in place, use on the end of the ribbon in Projects 8 and 13 to keep the ends from fraying.

Clothes pins, the kind that open and close with a spring hinge, help keep glued items in place until the glue is dry. You can find these in large discount stores, in the section that has laundry supplies.

Paint brushes in a variety of sizes are great for applying decoupage or glue in places where you need to be careful about how much you apply, and of course, paint brushes are good for painting.

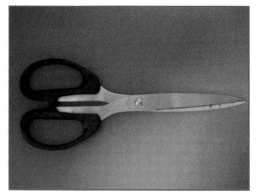

Scissors come in handy for many tasks during the jewelry making process. Be sure you have a sturdy pair, good for cutting through thick paper and yarn. You can find specialty scissors in a jewelry making catalog or store, but you can also just use the ones in a home sewing kit or kitchen drawer.

Keep scrap paper in a folder or large plastic bag. You can use large pieces, such as old newspapers, to cover your work space. Always keep all of the scraps from your other projects because you will probably need a small piece of a certain color in the future, and it's good to have small scraps handy.

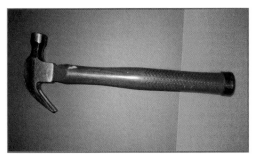

Hammers come in many sizes. If you are getting a hammer to add to your toolbox, visit the hardware store and purchase one that is smaller than a normal one. You can also just use a regular old hammer like the one that's used to hammer nails. If you borrow one from a parent or from someone else's toolbox or the garage, make sure that you return it where it belongs! When you hammer nails, use a pair of pliers to hold the nail in place while starting to hammer it. Watch out for fingers!

Nails come in many lengths and thicknesses. It's good to keep several sizes on hand for different projects. Find these in the garage, a "clutter" drawer in the kitchen, or in a parent's toolbox.

Scrap wood is used in Project 9. You do not need a large piece of wood; take a look around the garage or storage space and see if you find a leftover piece from a woodworking project. Many hardware stores sell bundles of scrap wood pieces at very low prices.

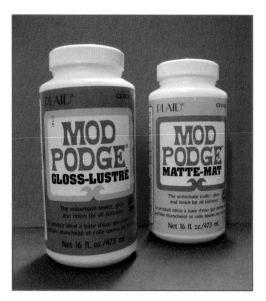

Decoupage glue is used as a protective coating for some surfaces. It can also be used as glue to hold things together. Use in multiple layers to get a thick protective layer. This glue goes on white and dries clear. It comes in either a glossy (shiny) or matte (not shiny) finish.

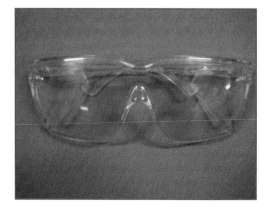

Safety goggles are not very stylish, but they are certainly necessary! Make it a habit to wear safety glasses to protect your eyes from flying bits of metal when you are cutting and from long wire flipping around and hitting you in the eye when you are bending it. Add your own artistic touch to these. Craft glue and rhinestones will give your goggles a touch of whimsy and individuality!

PROJECT 1

This is a great project to use for fundraising. Older kids can make these halos ahead of time and they can be sold pre-made. They also make a great activity to entertain younger kids or as a group project for a sleepover. The project shown here can be made with various colored chenille stems or different colors and shapes of sequins. Let your imagination run free with color schemes, shapes, and holiday themes.

Forest Fairy Halo

MATERIALS NEEDED

6 brown chenille stems
48 assorted leaf sequins
4 plastic flower shapes

TOOLS NEEDED

Wire cutters or old scissors
1/16" hole punch
Marker

1 Connect two chenille stems by twisting the ends together to form a circle. You can adjust the size of the halo at this time. Set the halo aside.

2 With the wire cutters or old scissors, cut two chenille stems into four equal pieces; you will have eight pieces total. Set these aside.

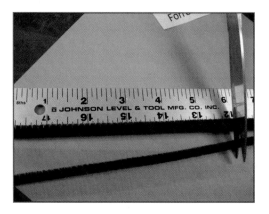 

3 Using the 1/16" hole punch, punch holes into the leaf sequins. The project pictured here uses 24 light green sequins and 24 dark green sequins for a total of 48 leaf sequins.

4 Use the eight pieces of chenille stems that you cut and the 48 leaf sequins that have holes punched into them to form branches to bend around the halo circle. First, slide two leaf sequins, one of each green shade, onto the chenille stem. Slide them down about an inch. Slide another leaf sequin onto the end of the chenille stem and bend the end of the stem over to keep the leaf sequin from coming off the stem. Slide the two leaf sequins that are on the chenille stem back up to where the end leaf sequin is attached. Repeat this step on the other end of the chenille stem. Alternate the light and dark green colors on the end leaf sequins. Do this to all eight of the cut chenille stems.

5 Put the halo that you made on a flat surface and lay the chenille stems with the leaf sequins on them around the halo. This will help you figure out where to put the stems.

6 Fold the chenille stems in the middle and wrap them around the halo twice to secure them in place. Once you have attached all eight stems with leaves to the halo, set this aside.

7 Using wire cutters or old scissors, cut two chenille stems in half. You will need four pieces approximately 6 inches long.

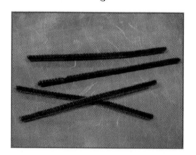

8 Curl the chenille stems around a marker to form curly vines to add to the halo. Do this to all four chenille stems.

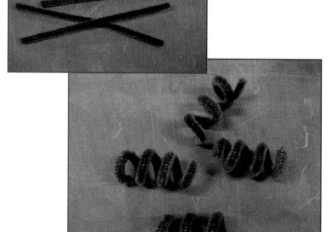

9 Slide one plastic flower onto one end of the curled chenille stem and bend the end to secure the flower in place. Leave the other end curly. Repeat this step for all of the curled chenille stems.

10 Decide where you want the flowers on the halo and attach them the same way that you attached the chenille stems with the leaf sequins, bending the curled chenille stems around the halo to secure them in place.

Sequins come in a wide variety of colors and shapes, so have fun, mix them up, and create your own designs.

PROJECT 2

These are great to make in many colors and sizes, and can also be a great fundraising idea. There are instructions for many different designs available online and in art and craft stores. This is a very easy beginning friendship bracelet.

Braided Friendship Bracelet

MATERIALS NEEDED

Three different colors of embroidery thread—enough of each to wrap around your wrist three times

TOOLS NEEDED

Scissors
Ruler
Tape

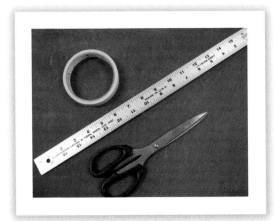

1 Choose three colors of thread to use for your bracelet. Wrap the thread around your wrist three times—this will tell you the length that you need for your finished bracelet. Cut the three threads to the right length.

2 Hold all three threads together and tie an overhand knot approximately 2 1/2 to 3 inches from the end of the threads.

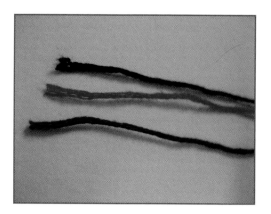

3 To keep the threads in place while you braid them, you can have a friend hold the end. If you're working alone, you can tape the ends to a counter top or tack the knot to a cork board.

4 Braid the three threads until the bracelet is long enough and then tie an overhand knot at the end of the braiding. Trim the "tail" of the threads to 2^1/$_2$ to 3 inches.

5 Wrap around your wrist, tie the ends together, and you're done!

You can find instructions for many ways to braid, from a simple three-strand braid, just as you would braid your hair, to more complex braids that use five or more strands of thread. Do a Google search for "braid" and check out all the results you'll find. You might want to start with a simple three-strand braid and then challenge yourself with the more complex varieties.

PROJECT 3

These fun bracelets can also be made as choker necklaces or ankle bracelets. Love Beads are a flashback to the 60s and 70s; ask your parents to help you make these; they probably remember how to do it! These will look great worn in multiples with many colors and sizes. You can also trade them with your friends. They are a good project for a sleepover or rainy afternoon.

Love and Friendship Beads

MATERIALS NEEDED

Assorted seed or E beads
Extra thin elastic beading cord

> E beads are larger than seed beads and smaller than pony beads. Find them at your favorite craft store.

TOOLS NEEDED

Ruler
Scissors
Tape
Beading needle
Industrial strength craft glue
Marker

1 Wrap a length of elastic cord around your wrist and mark it, and then add approximately four inches to that length. Make sure that you wrap the elastic cord loosely around your wrist. Do not stretch it tightly.

2 With scissors, cut the elastic cord to the size that you need.

3 Fold a piece of tape around one end of the elastic cord; this will keep the beads from sliding off.

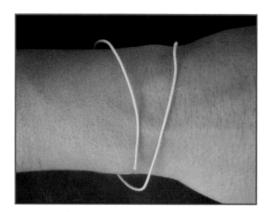

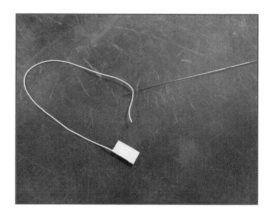

4 Use the beading needle to string the E beads onto the elastic cord. Open the eye of the beading needle and slide approximately 1 inch of the elastic cord through it.

5 Begin to thread the beads onto the beading needle and elastic cord. You can use one color, or you can make a pattern of two or more colors.

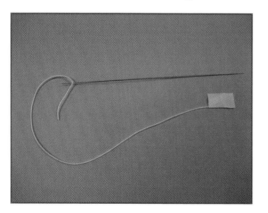

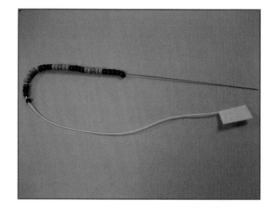

6 Continue to add beads until you have the elastic cord filled to the length that you want the bracelet to be.

7 Tie the ends of the elastic cord together. Place a dab of glue on the knot and let it dry before you trim the ends.

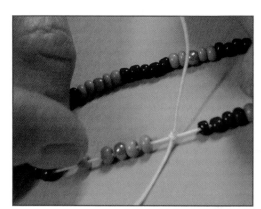

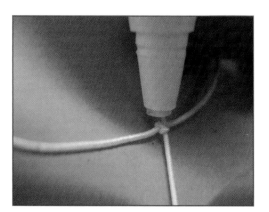

To make a choker, follow the same steps you used to make the bracelet, wrapping the elastic cord loosely around your neck and adding four extra inches. For an ankle bracelet, wrap the elastic cord loosely around your ankle and add four inches to the length.

PROJECT 4

Best Friends Forever! Check out the scrapbook section of your local craft store to find these round metal-edged paper tags. Then select a sticker to fit inside the metal edge of the tags. Stickers come in a variety of colors and styles. The necklace we make in this chapter uses clear stickers that come printed with letters of the alphabet. Spell a short word, a name, or...make one for your BFF!

B.F.F. Tag You're It! Necklace

MATERIALS NEEDED

Metal edged round tags
Letter stickers
Colorful lanyard clasps
Chain with clasp and links large enough for lanyard hooks to fit through

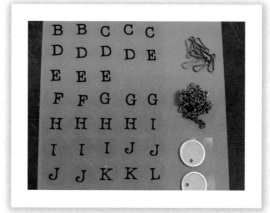

TOOLS NEEDED

1/16" hole punch

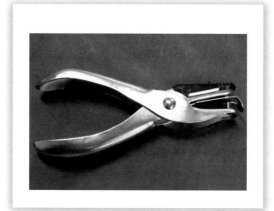

1 The stickers used for this project are a size that fits neatly inside the metal edge of the tags. All you need to do is peel the sticker from the backing and apply it to the tag.

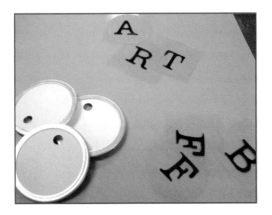

2 Use the hole punch to make holes in the tags.

3 Slide the lanyard hook through the holes in the letter tags. You can use the same color for all the tags or you can create a color scheme using your favorite mixture of colors.

4 Find the center of the chain and slide the lanyard hook through the center link of the necklace. To evenly space the letter tags, count approx six or seven links to each side of the center tag and attach the other letter tags.

Use your initials, name, or any other short word. You can add beaded head pins to the links between the letter tags (described in Chapter 15, "Bead Drop Earrings"). You can also cut pictures from old magazines or print out pictures or letters on the computer and use white craft glue or decoupage glue to attach them to the surface of the tags.

PROJECT 5

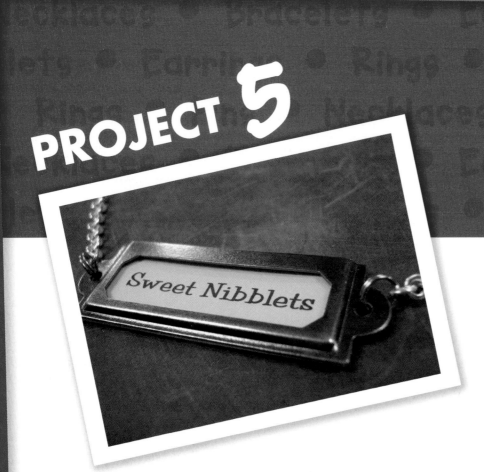

Sweet Nibblets

This project makes a great gift. Try making several different labels so that they can be changed. You can also use patterned paper with your name printed on it for the label. Or try using your school or mascot name or your favorite sports team.

Label Holder
Necklace

MATERIALS NEEDED

Metal label holder
Small piece of poster board or matte board
Printed label or picture
Chain with clasp
2 split jump rings

TOOLS NEEDED

Ruler
Marker
Scissors
Industrial strength craft glue
Wire cutters
2 clothes pins (optional)

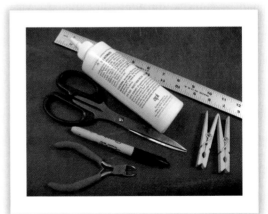

1 Turn the label holder over and measure the back side of it. Measure and mark the poster or matte board. With scissors, cut the piece of poster or matte board to fit on the back of the label holder.

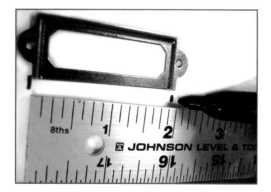 

2 Check the fit of the cut piece of poster or matte board and trim it if you need to. Place a small amount of industrial strength craft glue around the three edges of the label holder, leaving the opening at the top of the label holder without glue. You can use clothes pins on each end of the holder to keep the poster or matte board in place while the glue is drying. Set this aside.

 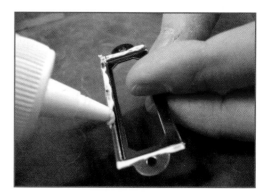

3 Find the center of your chain and use wire cutters to cut and remove a link from the chain.

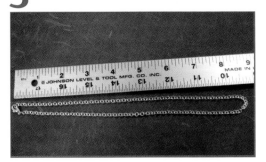

4 Split jump rings are like tiny split key chains. Attach one split jump ring to each end link of the chain.

5 Attach one split jump ring with chain to one side of the label holder. Repeat on the other side of the label holder. Set this aside.

6 Use a computer to print a name or word using your favorite font onto a colorful piece of paper. You could also cut a picture or words out of an old magazine.

7 Use the measurements that you used when you cut the poster or matte board and cut the paper for your label slightly smaller than those measurements.

8 Slide the cut paper into the label holder and you are ready to go!

PROJECT 6

Mix your favorite colors and bead combinations for this quick and easy project. You can find all kinds of beads at local craft and hobby stores, such as Michael's or Hobby Lobby.

Leather Cord and Donut Bead Necklace

MATERIALS NEEDED

Leather cord
Assorted beads
Large donut bead
Chunky glass beads with
large holes

TOOLS NEEDED

Ruler
Marker
Scissors

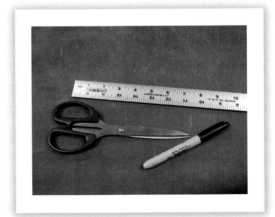

1 Measure and cut the leather cord to 34 inches.

2 Fold the cord in half.

3 Place both ends of the cord through the hole in the donut bead. Run the two ends of the cord through the loop at the center of the folded leather cord.

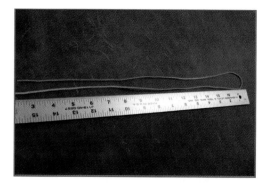

Search for unique and original beads and coordinate the cord color with the beads.

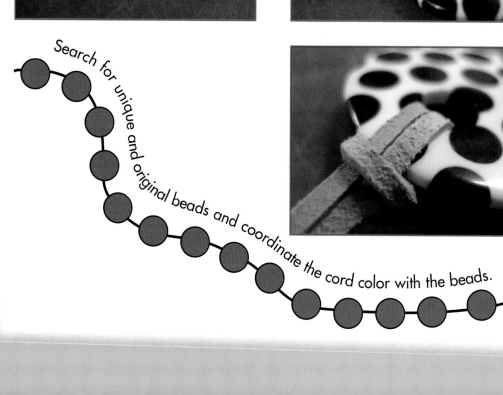

4 Slide both ends of the leather cord through the holes in the chunky beads and slide the chunky bead down to the donut bead.

5 Tie the ends of the cord into a knot.

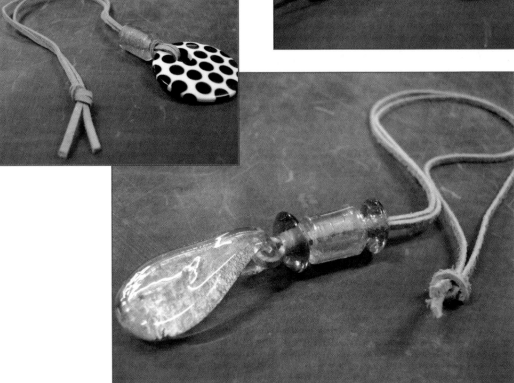

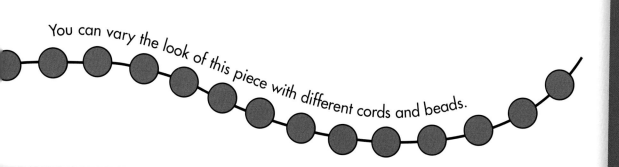

You can vary the look of this piece with different cords and beads.

PROJECT 7

Memory wire comes in many sizes: necklace, ring, small and large bracelet. It is a steel wire that is made to keep its circular shape. Make a matching set for all your friends. Add a charm or dangle to the necklace or the loop at each end of the bracelet to create a different look.

Memory Wire Bracelet

MATERIALS NEEDED

Bracelet size memory wire
Assorted beads

TOOLS NEEDED

Chain nose pliers
Round nose pliers

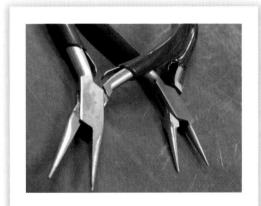

1 Determine the number of memory wire loops that you want to use for your bracelet.

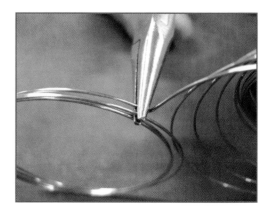

2 When working with memory wire, do not use cutters. Instead use chain nose or flat nose pliers to bend the wire back and forth to break it. It only requires a couple of bends to do this.

3 Use the round nose pliers to curl one end of the memory wire to form a loop (this will keep the beads from sliding off your bracelet). This wire is not easy to bend, so it may take a few attempts to get the loop closed.

4 Start placing beads onto the end of the memory wire. Use seed beads, E beads, or larger beads. Keep in mind that larger beads will make the bracelet heavier.

5 Leave approximately 1/2 inch of wire unbeaded at the end to allow enough wire to curl around and form another loop.

6 Use the round nose pliers to form a loop at the other end, and your bracelet is complete!

PROJECT 8

This bracelet is a great accessory to brighten every outfit. Spritz the flower with a sweet smelling fragrance so that it will look good and smell good. You can make a choker to match your bracelet or one to go around your ankle. This bracelet will look great with your swimsuit on the beach!

Ribbon and Silk Flower Bracelet

MATERIALS NEEDED

Grosgrain ribbon
Hook and loop closure with sticky back
Silk flowers
Brad

> You could use felt flowers instead of silk ones, or flowers of any material you choose.

TOOLS NEEDED

Ruler
Marker
Scissors
White craft glue
Piece of scrap paper
Clothes pins

1 To determine the length of ribbon that will be needed for your bracelet, cut a strip of paper the same width as the ribbon you are using for the bracelet. Wrap the paper around your wrist and mark the length that is needed to fit around your wrist. Add approximately 1 1/2 inches to that length to allow extra ribbon to fold over at each end of the bracelet where the hook and loop closure will be attached.

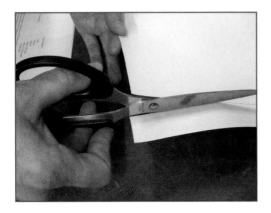
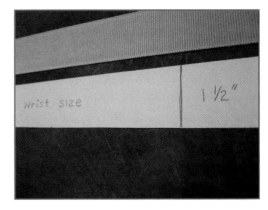

2 Cut the ribbon to length. Wrap the ribbon around your wrist to make sure the ribbon overlaps at least 1 1/2 inches.

3 Spread a small amount of white craft glue onto each end of the ribbon to prevent fraying.

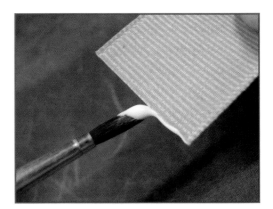

4 Fold each end of the ribbon over approximately 3/4 inch and glue the ends in place. Use your finger or an old paint brush to spread the glue evenly over the ends of the ribbon. After you have folded the ends of the ribbon over and applied the glue, use clothes pins to keep the folded ribbon in place until it is dry.

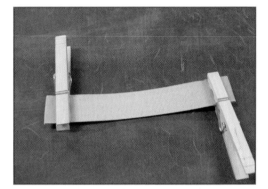

5 Choose colorful silk flowers and, if necessary, remove the stem and the plastic center of the flowers. You can layer different color flowers for a dramatic effect.

6 After you remove the plastic center of the flowers, a small hole will be left in the center of the flower. Place the pointed end of the brad through the holes in the flowers. Split the two sides of the brad open and bend them flat against the back side of the flowers.

7 Use white craft glue and attach the flower to the center of the ribbon. After applying the flower to the ribbon with the glue you can use a clothes pin to keep the flower in place while the glue dries.

8 Apply the sticky backed hook and loop circle to each end of the ribbon where you have folded it over. Make sure that they are applied on the right side of the ribbon so that the bracelet will close properly.

9 Make sure that the glue has dried thoroughly before wearing your bracelet. Letting the glue dry overnight is a good idea!

Pre-made leather bracelets come in many colors, textures, and sizes. The metal brads used in this piece come in many shapes, colors, and sizes. In this project, we used the wearer's initials, but you can find brads with fun shapes, numbers, and lots more.

Leather Bracelet with Brads

MATERIALS NEEDED

Leather bracelet with snaps
Assorted brads

TOOLS NEEDED

Scrap piece of paper
Pencil, pen, or marker
Scissors
Ruler
1/16 hole punch
Nail
Hammer
Scrap piece of wood

The best way to make sure that the holes are in the correct place on the leather bracelet is to make a paper pattern. You can use the pattern to make sure that the brads are spaced evenly and the holes are marked in the correct place.

1 To make a paper pattern, lay the leather bracelet flat on a piece of scrap paper and trace around it with a pencil, pen, or marker.

2 Cut the paper on the line that you traced around the leather bracelet.

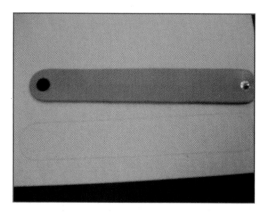

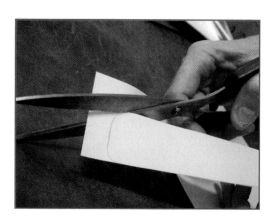

3 Decide on the number and size of the brads that you want to use on the bracelet.

4 Place the brads flat side down on the paper bracelet pattern and use them to determine the distance that you want between the brads. If you are using an odd number of brads, measure the center of the bracelet and work your way out. Use the pencil and a ruler to make evenly spaced marks on the paper bracelet pattern at the center of each brad; these marks are where you will make the holes for the brads.

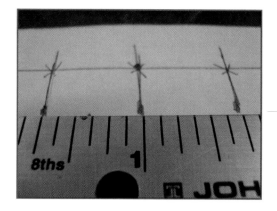

5 Use the 1/16 inch hole punch to make holes in the paper bracelet pattern where you measured and marked the holes for the brads to go.

6 Place the pointed ends of the brads through the holes that have been punched into the paper bracelet pattern, but do not split the pointed ends apart. This is when you decide if you like where the brads are and if you want to adjust the hole placement before you use the nail to make holes in the leather bracelet.

7 You may need to cut another paper bracelet pattern and try this a few times to get the holes where you need them. That's ok! That's why scrap paper was used!

8 When you're finally happy with where the brads will be placed, remove them from the paper bracelet pattern and set them aside.

9 Lay the paper bracelet pattern with the holes punched into it on top of the leather bracelet and mark the spots where you want to make the holes for the brads.

10 When you have all of the holes marked onto the leather bracelet, remove the paper bracelet pattern.

11 Lay the leather bracelet onto a scrap piece of wood. Place the point of a nail onto the bracelet where you made a mark for a hole. You can hold the nail with a pair of pliers to help keep the nail in place. Be careful of your fingers! You can also have a parent do this step for you. Hit the top of the nail with the hammer two or three times until the nail just starts to go through the bracelet—there will be a small hole through to the back side of it. Turn the bracelet over and use the hammer to hit the top of the nail. Place the nail on the small opening that you created from the front; this will make the hole large enough for the pointed ends of the brad to fit through. Repeat this step until there are holes in all the marked spots that you made for the brads to go through.

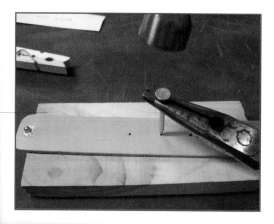

12 Place the pointed end of a brad through the first hole that you made. You can add a dab of glue under the flat head of the brad at this time if you wish. Split the two sides of the brad open and bend them flat against the back side of the leather bracelet. Repeat this for all of the brads.

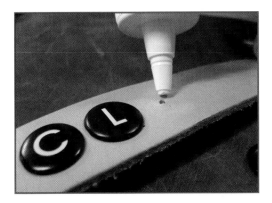 

The smaller the pointed part of the brads are, the smaller the size of nail you will need. The leather snap bracelets come in a variety of colors and sizes. You can use stamps and permanent ink to add color and patterns to the leather. Brads also come in a wide variety of colors, shapes, and sizes. Check out the local scrap booking store or local art and craft store for supplies.

You can use the same technique to decorate a purchased leather dog collar for your best four-legged friend.

This project uses metal plates stamped with an inspirational word. Choose a word that is meaningful to you and use your favorite color combinations when choosing beads for this project.

Beaded Inspiration Bracelet

MATERIALS NEEDED

.5mm clear, stretchy jewelry cord
Assorted seed or E beads
Metal plates with stamped
inspirational words

TOOLS NEEDED

Ruler
Marker
Scissors
Beading needle
Craft glue
Tape

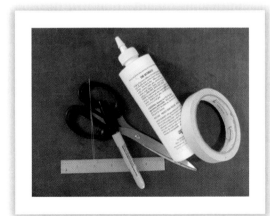

1 Wrap a piece of stretchy cord around your wrist twice and add approximately 5" to that length. Make sure that you wrap the stretchy cord loosely around your wrist. Do not stretch the cord.

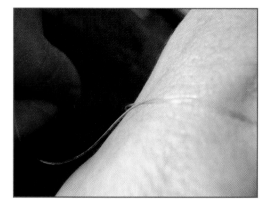

2 With scissors, cut the stretchy cord to the size that you need.

3 Fold the stretchy cord in half. First slide the two ends of the folded stretchy cord through the hole in the stamped metal plate, and then slide the two ends through the loop at the other end of the folded piece of stretchy cord. Secure in place with a knot. Slide an E bead through *both* cords next to the metal word plate.

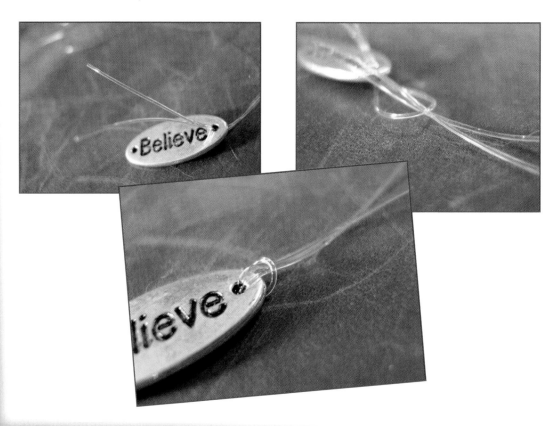

4 Now you'll use the beading needle to string the beads onto the stretchy cord. Open the eye of the beading needle and slide approximately 1" of one strand of the stretchy cord through the eye of the beading needle.

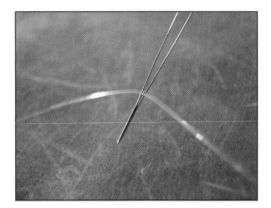

E beads, also known as Rocaille or seed, beads, are tiny glass beads. They come packaged in various colors and sizes. You can find them at any craft store, such as Michael's or Hobby Lobby, or at fabric stores like Jo-Ann Fabrics.

5 Begin to thread the beads onto the beading needle and one strand of the stretchy cord. Use one color of beads, or use mixed colors and decide on a pattern in which to use them.

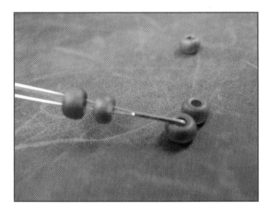

6 Continue to add beads until you have the stretchy cord filled to the length that you want the bracelet to be. You can lay the stamped metal plate on top of your wrist and slide the beaded stretchy cord with beads through the hole in the stamped metal plate to check the fit of the bracelet. Add more beads to make it longer or remove beads to make it shorter.

7 When you have enough beads on one side of the stretchy cord to fill it to the length it needs to be, remove the end of the stretchy cord from the beading needle and fold a piece of tape on the end of the cord to keep the beads from sliding off.

8 Using the beading needle, fill the other strand of the stretchy cord with beads. When you have the correct number of beads on both cords, remove the tape from the first cord. Slide the end of one strand of the stretchy cord through the hole in the metal plate and loop the cord through twice. Do the same with the other strand of the beaded stretchy cord. Slide the ends of both cords through the end E bead on each strand. Tie the ends of the cord together with an overhand knot. Place a small dab of glue on the knot and let it dry before you trim the ends.

The possible picture choices for this project are unlimited. Draw your own. Make black and white copies of a friend's photograph. Add names or dates. Print out meaningful quotes. Use a picture on both sides of the wood shape to create a two-sided necklace.

Wood Decoupage Necklace

MATERIALS NEEDED

Thin wooden shape with hole drilled
Acrylic paint
Picture from old magazine
Cord or ribbon
Chunky bead

TOOLS NEEDED

Paint brush
Ruler
Marker
Scissors
Scrap paper, wax paper, or newspaper
Decoupage glue

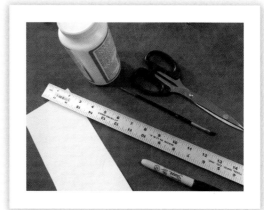

1 A great way to see how the picture will look on the wood shape is to make a pattern. Place the wood shape on a scrap piece of paper and trace around the wood shape, making sure to mark the spot where the hole is drilled.

2 Draw a smaller shape in the middle of the paper pattern. This will be a "window" to see how the picture will look on the wood shape.

3 Carefully cut the smaller shape from the paper pattern of the wood shape.

4 Find an old magazine and look through it for colorful pictures to use. Place the paper pattern over the pictures to see how they will look. Use the pattern to draw the lines for cutting out the picture. You can also use clip art or words printed from a computer for the necklace.

5 Cut the picture out and set it aside.

6 Decide what color to use on the wood shape as the background color.

7 Cover your work surface with wax paper, newspaper, or scrap paper. Paint the wood shape on the front, back, and edges. Acrylic paint dries quickly and cleans up easily with water. Make sure that the paint is thoroughly rinsed from the paint brush when you're done.

8 After the paint is dry, decide on the placement of the picture. It's best to decide ahead of time where you want the picture because once you apply the decoupage glue, the picture will be difficult to move around.

9 Use the paint brush to cover the surface of the painted wood shape with a thin coat of decoupage glue. While the decoupage glue is still wet, lay the picture in place. Use the paint brush to cover the picture and painted wood shape with another thin layer of decoupage glue. Allow the front to thoroughly dry and then use the paint brush to apply a thin layer of decoupage glue to the back and edges of the wood shape. Allow the back and edges to thoroughly dry.

10 Once the decoupage glue on the front, back, and edges is dry, slide the cord through the hole in the wood shape. Slide the wood shape to the middle of the cord. Place both ends of the cord through the hole in the chunky bead and slide the bead down to the top of the wood shape.

11 Tie the ends into a knot and the necklace is done!

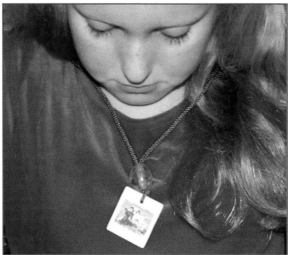

Many colors of hemp cord are available so you can make this piece in lots of different color combinations. Add more knots or more beads to the design. Allow extra cord if you will be using lots of knots in your design. This is a great item to make for fundraising.

Colorful Beads and Hemp Cord Necklace

MATERIALS NEEDED

Hemp cord
Assorted large and small beads

TOOLS NEEDED

Ruler
Scissors
Marker

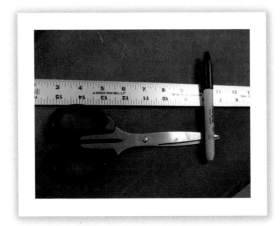

1 Measure and cut a 36" length of the hemp cord.

2 Measure and mark the center of the hemp cord. All of the marks that you make on the cord will be covered up by beads.

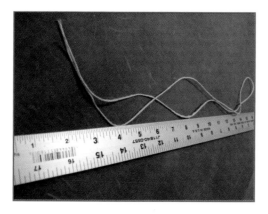

3 Tie a knot in the hemp cord just to the side of the center mark. Add one large bead to the cord and tie another knot in the hemp cord on the other side of the bead.

4 Measure two inches from the knot and mark the hemp cord. Repeat this on the other side of the necklace. This will help to keep the bead spacing even on the necklace.

5 Tie a knot in the hemp cord close to the 2" mark that you made on it.

6 Slide three small beads onto the cord and make another knot in the cord on the other side of the beads. Repeat this on the other side of the necklace.

7 Measure another two inches up from the last knot and mark the cord on each side of the necklace.

8 Add a large bead to each side of the necklace before you knot the cord. Slide the large bead to the knot above the three small beads. Repeat this on the other side of the necklace.

9 Tie a knot in the cord close to the two inch mark that you made two inches from the knot above the three beads.

10 Add one small bead, one large bead, and then another small bead. Tie another knot in the cord above the small bead. Repeat this on the other side of the necklace.

11 Measure another two inches up from the last knot and mark the cord on each side of the necklace.

12 Tie a knot in the cord close to the 2" mark that you made on the cord.

13 Add nine small beads to the cord and tie a knot in the cord above the last small bead. Repeat this on the other side of the necklace.

14 Knot the two ends of the cord together and you are done!

This is a great vacation or after vacation project. Choose some sand from your special vacation spot, and send this message in a bottle to someone special who couldn't join you on vacation. Create your own special piece to evoke memories to have with you all year long. This would also make a great beach party themed activity.

Message in a Bottle Necklace

MATERIALS NEEDED

Glass bottle for the message
Sand
Paper for the note
Ribbon
One 6mm jump ring
E beads
Shell with hole

TOOLS NEEDED

Ruler
Marker
Two pairs of chain nose pliers
Craft glue
Scissors

1 Gently remove the stopper from the glass bottle. Wiggle it a little bit if it is hard to get out. If the eye screw becomes loose or comes out while you are trying to remove the cork, use craft glue and place the eye screw back into the hole that it came out of. Then set the stopper aside to dry.

2 Decide on the message that you want to place inside the bottle. Write the message on a piece of paper, roll it up tightly, and insert the paper into the bottle. Make sure that the paper is short enough so that the cork can be replaced into the bottle. If you need to remove the message for any reason, you can use tweezers to get it out of the bottle.

3 Pour a small amount of sand into the bottle and replace the cork. You can also add really, really, small sea shells if you can find them. Set this aside.

4 Open the jump ring.

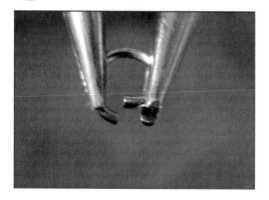

Opening and closing jump rings:

With two pair of chain nose pliers pointing up, hold the jump ring with the opening at the top. Roll one of your wrists away from you and your other wrist toward you, opening the jump ring only as much as you need to. To close the jump ring, hold it the same way and roll your wrists in the opposite direction. Think of holding a piece of paper and tearing it! Never pull the jump ring ends out; this will weaken the metal, and it will be difficult to close the jump ring.

5 Add three E beads to the jump ring and then slide the jump ring through the hole in the shell. Close the jump ring. Set this aside.

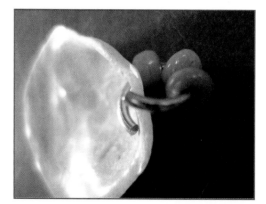

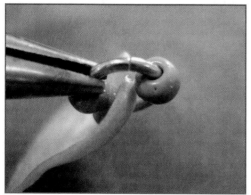

6 Use the ruler to measure and mark a 30" length of ribbon. Use scissors to cut the ribbon.

7 Apply a small amount of craft glue to each end of the ribbon to prevent it from fraying. Set the ribbon aside to dry.

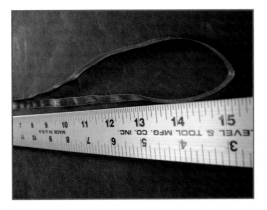

8 When the glue on the ends of the ribbon is dry (this won't take long), slide the ribbon through the loop of the eye pin on the top of the bottle. Slide the bottle to the center of the ribbon. Approximately 2 inches up from the bottle tie an overhand knot with both strands of the ribbon. Then slide the jump ring with the shell and beads onto one of the ribbons and tie another knot to hold the jump ring in place.

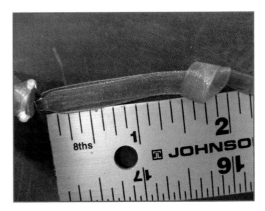

9 Tie an overhand knot at the end of the ribbons and now you have a great handmade vacation souvenir necklace.

Put your necklace in a padded envelope and send one to your BFF back home.

This great wire spiral design is fun and easy to make. Play with the spiral sizes and come up with a fun combination of your own. Wire comes in many colors, so use your imagination and design your own unique spiral ring using different size and color combinations.

Wire Spiral Ring

MATERIALS NEEDED

18-gauge colored wire

TOOLS NEEDED

Masking tape
Chain nose pliers
Round nose pliers
Ruler
Marker
Wire cutters
Safety glasses

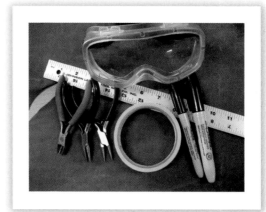

1 The first thing you must do is determine what size ring will fit your finger. Make your loops for the ring shank to match a ring that you know fits the finger that you want to wear the spiral ring on. Then use a round object that is similar in size to the ring. A thick marker might be just the thing!

2 To keep the pliers from making marks on the colored wire, wrap the ends of the pliers with masking tape.

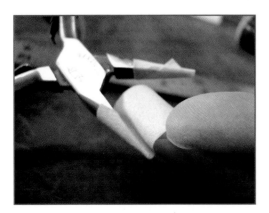
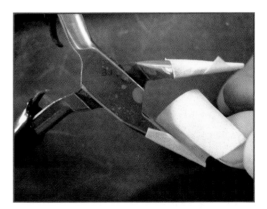

It is very important to wear safety glasses when working with wire. Avoid eye injury!

3 Before you cut the wire from the spool, use the round nose pliers to form a small loop at the end of the wire. Hold the loop that you formed in the jaws of the chain nose pliers and continue to bend into a spiral until it is approximately the size of a pencil eraser. Unroll the wire from the spool and lay the wire flat on a ruler. Measure approximately 13 inches of wire and, using wire cutters, cut the wire.

4 Form a small loop at the end of the wire that you cut from the spool. Hold the loop that you formed in the jaws of the chain nose pliers and continue to bend the wire into a spiral until it is approximately the size of a pencil eraser.

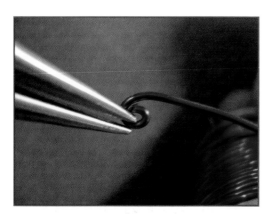

I always recommend making the end spirals first so that you are not working with a long piece of wire with a pointed end.

5 Measure and mark the center of the wire. Place the center mark on the marker (or whatever round object you are using to size the ring) and begin to wrap the wire around it. When you have wrapped the wire so that you have four wires on the back of the ring, twist the two wires with the spiral ends together to keep them in place.

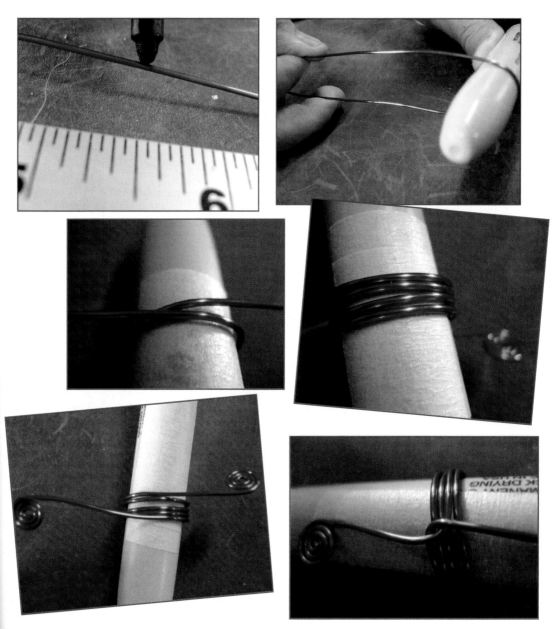

6 Use the chain nose pliers to finish bending the wire into the spirals. You can adjust the placement of the spirals on the ring to get the look you want.

Use two strands of different colored wire to make four colorful spirals. You will need two pieces of wire approximately 7 inches long after you have formed the end spirals. Use 18- or 20-gauge wire. 18-gauge wire is thicker and will keep its shape better.

When making these basic bead earrings if you choose beads that match the ones used on the memory wire bracelet in Project 7, you will have earrings that match your bracelet. Add the necklace from Project 16 and you'll have a matching three-piece set!

Bead Drop Earrings

MATERIALS NEEDED

Two 1 1/2" head pins (I use base metal.)

Assorted beads

Two sterling silver ear wires

TOOLS NEEDED

Ruler

Marker

Wire cutters or tin snips

Chain nose pliers

Round nose pliers

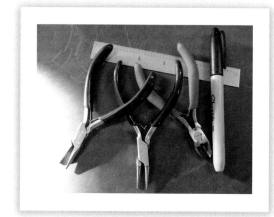

1 Slide the beads onto the head pin.

2 Use the ruler to measure and mark 5/16 inch above the top bead on the head pin. With the wire cutters or tin snips, cut the head pin wire 5/16 inch above the top bead.

3 Using the chain nose pliers, bend the head pin wire next to the top bead at a 90-degree, or right, angle.

4 Hold the head pin with the beads on it in one hand with the wire that you bent pointing toward you. Using the round nose pliers, grip the end of the head pin wire that is pointing toward you and roll it away from you. Your hand position will be similar to that of holding a bicycle handle bar. Release the head pin wire with the pliers. At this point, the opening in the loop at the top of the head pin wire should still be large enough to slip the ear wire on. After you add the ear wire, use the round nose pliers to grasp the loop of the head pin wire and roll it closed. If needed, you can use the round nose pliers or chain nose pliers to adjust the shape of your loop at the top of the head pin.

5 Repeat these steps for the second earring. It will become easier to keep the loop round in shape the more that you do this technique.

I use base metal head pins for strength on projects that use a loop closure at the top. Base metal is stronger than sterling silver, and you will not need to worry about the loop coming open. I use sterling silver for the ear wires because some people are sensitive to base metal when it comes into direct contact with their skin. Using sterling silver ear wires is also a good selling point if you want to sell your jewelry.

This basic bead necklace can be made to match the memory wire bracelet in Project 7 or the earrings in Project 15. You can use colored leather, a chain, satin cord, or a ribbon to hang the bead drop from. There are many options available at your local craft and hobby store.

Bead Drop Necklace

MATERIALS NEEDED

One 1 1/2" head pins (I use base
metal.)
Assorted beads
Chain with clasp

TOOLS NEEDED

Ruler
Marker
Wire cutters or tin snips
Chain nose pliers
Round nose pliers

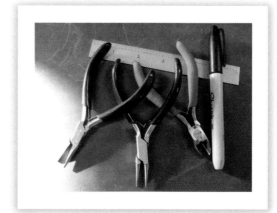

1 Slide the beads onto the head pin.

2 Use the ruler to measure and mark $1/2$ inch above the top bead on the head pin. With the wire cutters or tin snips, cut the head pin wire $1/2$ inch above the top bead.

3 Using the chain nose pliers, bend the head pin wire next to the top bead at a 90-degree, or right, angle.

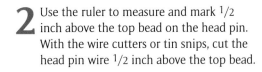

4 Hold the head pin with the beads on it in one hand with the wire that you bent pointing toward you. Using the round nose pliers, grip the end of the head pin wire that is pointing toward you and roll it away from you. Your hand position will be similar to that of holding a bicycle handle bar. Release the head pin wire with the pliers. Use the round nose pliers to grasp the loop of the head pin wire and roll the loop closed. If needed, you can use the round nose pliers or chain nose pliers to adjust the shape of your loop at the top of the head pin.

5 Slide the loop at the top of the beaded head pin onto the chain.

You can make several of these in different colors and styles; they can be interchanged on the cord to match many outfits. You can add one to a keychain. This necklace is a best seller for fundraising projects, too.

INDEX

Inspiration from Some Working Artists

Laura Villanyi, glass bead artist:

"Learn, practice, learn, practice, practice, practice, practice, and practice some more."

"Enjoy creating with your hands."

"Bring an open mind to the easel."

"Take pride in your craftsmanship."

Anna Villanyi, student of the arts!

"Focus on what you are doing."

"Don't worry about making mistakes when you begin, just keep making."

"Being perfect is a waste of time."

The Art Collector*

A famous art collector is walking through the city when he notices a mangy cat lapping milk from a saucer in the doorway of a store. He does a double take.

He knows that the saucer is extremely old and very valuable, so he walks casually into the store and offers to buy the cat for two dollars.

The store owner replies, "I'm sorry, but the cat isn't for sale."

The collector says, "Please, I need a hungry cat around the house to catch mice. I'll pay you 20 dollars for the cat." At that, the owner says "Sold," and hands over the cat.

The collector continues, "Hey, for the 20 bucks I wonder if you could throw in that old saucer. The cat's used to it, and it'll save me from having to get a dish."

The owner says, "Sorry, buddy, but that's my lucky saucer. So far this week, I've sold 68 cats.

Famous Artist Quotes

Jim Davis, creator of Garfield

"There are so many opportunities in life that the loss of two or three capabilities is not necessarily debilitating. A handicap can give you the opportunity to focus more on art, writing, or music."

"Way down deep, we're all motivated by the same urges. Cats have the courage to live by them."

FUN FACT
There are no words in the dictionary that rhyme with: orange, purple, and silver.

Walt Disney

"The way to get started is to quit talking and begin doing."

"You can dream it, you can do it."

"It all started with a mouse."

* Short story from basicjokes.com

Georgia O'Keeffe
"I found I could say things with color and shapes that I couldn't say any other way—things I had no words for."

Quentin Tarantino
"I don't think there's anything to be afraid of. Failure brings great rewards—in the life of an artist."

Andy Warhol
"An artist is someone who produces things that people don't need to have but that he—for some reason—thinks it would be a good idea to give to them."

Scott Adams
"Creativity is allowing yourself to make mistakes. Art is knowing which ones to keep."

Pablo Picasso
"All children are artists. The problem is how to remain an artist once he grows up."
"Everything you can imagine is real."
"God is really only another artist. He invented the giraffe, the elephant, and the cat. He has no real style; He just goes on trying other things."

Saul Bellow
"What is art but a way of seeing?"

Jedi Master Yoda
"Truly wonderful, the mind of a child."

Dr. Theodore Seuss Geisel
"Today is your day; your mountain is waiting. So… get on your way."
"Think left and think right and think low and think high. Oh, the thinks you can think up if only you try."

Unknown
"It is not hard to understand modern art: If it hangs on the wall, it's a painting; if you can walk around it, it's a sculpture."

Degas
"Painting is easy when you don't know how, but very difficult when you do."

Albert Einstein
"Imagination is more important that knowledge. Knowledge is limited. Imagination encircles the world."

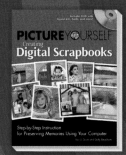

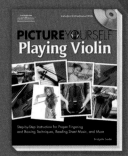

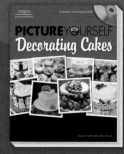

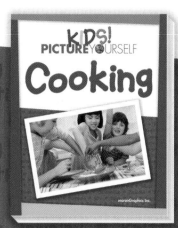
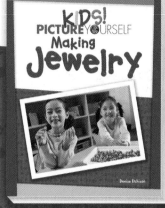
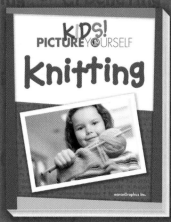
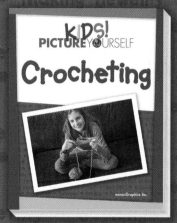